Our Nation's Pride

The Statue of Liberty

By Darlene R. Stille
Illustrated by Todd Ouren

Content Consultant:
Richard Jensen, Ph.D.
Author, Scholar, and Historian

magic
wagon

Visit us at www.abdopublishing.com

Published by Magic Wagon, a division of the ABDO Publishing Group, 8000 West 78th Street, Edina, Minnesota 55439.

Printed in the United States.

Text by Darlene R. Stille
Illustrations by Todd Ouren
Edited by Patricia Stockland
Interior layout and design by Nicole Brecke
Cover design by Nicole Brecke

Library of Congress Cataloging-in-Publication Data
Stille, Darlene R.
  The Statue of Liberty / Darlene Stille ; illustrated by Todd Ouren ; content consultant, Richard Jensen.
     p. cm. — (Our nation's pride)
  Includes bibliographical references and index.
  ISBN 978-1-60270-115-1
  1. Statue of Liberty (New York, N.Y.)—Juvenile literature. 2. New York (N.Y.)—Buildings, structures, etc.—Juvenile literature. I. Ouren, Todd. II. Jensen, Richard J. III. Title.
F128.64.L6S75 2008
974.7'1--dc22
                            2007034065

Table of Contents

A Big Statue

There is a huge statue in New York Harbor.

It is called the Statue of Liberty. It looks like a lady.

She is wearing a long robe and a crown. She is

holding up a glowing torch in her right hand.

The Statue of Liberty is a symbol. It stands for

freedom. It stands for the United States of America.

United States
of America

France

A Wonderful Gift

The Statue of Liberty was a gift from the people of France. In the 1700s, the French helped the Americans fight for freedom. Citizens of both countries loved liberty. So, the French wanted to show their friendship with a gift.

A Great Idea

The idea to build the statue came from a man in France. His name was Édouard de Laboulaye. He told his friends about his idea.

One friend was a sculptor. A sculptor is a kind of artist. Sculptors make statues and other things. The sculptor's name was Frédéric Bartholdi. Frédéric said he would build a statue.

What Kind of Statue?

Frédéric wanted to build the biggest statue in the world! He started with modeling clay. He made a small statue that he liked.

Next, Frédéric went to New York. He picked a place to put the statue. The place was a small island. Then, he went back to France and built the statue there.

Building the Statue

Frédéric and his helpers started the statue in 1875.

First, they carved wood to look like parts of the statue.

Next, they laid copper sheets on the wood. Then, they

hit the copper sheets with hammers to shape them.

They shaped some copper sheets to look like the torch.

They shaped others to look like the head.

The Pedestal

The Statue of Liberty stands on top of a building.

The building is called the pedestal. Americans began

the building while the statue was being created. They

built it on the island in New York Harbor. The island is

now called Liberty Island.

Materials for the Statue

The Statue of Liberty is made of 300 thin sheets of copper. Pennies are also made of copper. The copper sheets for the statue are about as thick as two pennies.

The copper sheets could not stand alone. There is a strong tower inside the statue. The tower is made of iron and steel. The copper sheets are fastened to the tower.

The Statue Goes to New York

When the statue was finished, it was taken apart.

Frédéric's helpers put the pieces in wooden boxes.

They needed 214 boxes. Then, Frédéric sent the statue

to the United States.

Americans put the parts together on Liberty Island.

First, they put up a tower. Then, they fastened the

copper sheets to the iron bars.

The statue was finished in 1886. It was as tall as a

22-story building!

What the Statue Means

Each part of the statue is a symbol. Seven spikes in the crown stand for the world's seven seas. They also stand for the seven continents. The torch stands for the light of liberty. A broken chain at the statue's feet stands for freedom.

The statue holds a tablet in her left arm.

Writing on the tablet says, "JULY IV MDCCLXXVI."

These letters stand for a date, July 4, 1776.

Americans signed the Declaration of Independence

on that day.

A Welcome Sight

People in other lands wanted to come to the United States to live. Millions of people left their homes. They sailed across the Atlantic Ocean.

The trip was long and hard. At last, they sailed into New York Harbor. The Statue of Liberty was there to welcome them.

Fixing the Statue

The Statue of Liberty stands outdoors. Rain and snow fell on it for almost 100 years. The iron bars rusted. The statue had to be fixed. It had to be cleaned. It needed new metal bars and a new torch. No one could visit it for two years.

The statue opened again on July 4, 1986. It was better than ever. Millions of people visit it every year. Its new torch flame is covered with gold. Big lights shine on the gold. The light makes the flame glow.

A Visit to the Statue

To visit the Statue of Liberty, you take a boat to Liberty Island. A ranger tells you about the statue. The ranger shows you a fort on Liberty Island.

There is a museum inside the pedestal. You can see the first torch there. An elevator can take you to the top of the pedestal. You can look at the harbor all around. From the Statue of Liberty, you can view the land of the free.

Fun Facts

• People love the Statue of Liberty. They have given it many names. Some call it "Lady Liberty." Some called it "Mother of Exiles." The real name of the statue is *Liberty Enlightening the World*.

• A French man named Gustave Eiffel helped make the Statue of Liberty. He built the tower that holds up the statue. He also built a famous tower in Paris. It is called the Eiffel Tower.

• How big is the statue? Each eye is 18 inches (46 cm) across. The mouth is 36 inches (91 cm) wide.

• The metal in the statue weighs 312,000 pounds (142 t). That weight is as much as 104 average family cars.

• The U.S. government owns Liberty Island.

Glossary

continent—a very large area of land. North America is a continent.

copper—an orange-colored metal.

Declaration of Independence—an essay written in 1776, announcing the separation of the American colonies from Great Britain.

iron—a kind of strong metal.

island—a small area of land in a lake or a sea.

museum—a place where visitors can see important objects of art, history, or science.

pedestal—a base that something sits on.

steel—a metal made with iron that does not easily rust.

symbol—something that stands for something else. On the Statue of Liberty, the torch is a symbol for the light of liberty.

On the Web

To learn more about the Statue of Liberty, visit ABDO Publishing Company on the World Wide Web at **www.abdopublishing.com**. Web sites about the Statue of Liberty are featured on our Book Links page. These links are routinely monitored and updated to provide the most current information available.

Index